Songs from an Earlier Century

Also by Ira Joe Fisher

Remembering Rew (2004)
Some Holy Weight in the Village Air (2006)

Songs from an Earlier Century

Ira Joe Fisher

The New York Quarterly Foundation, Inc.
New York, New York

NYQ Books™ is an imprint of The New York Quarterly Foundation, Inc.

The New York Quarterly Foundation, Inc.
P. O. Box 2015
Old Chelsea Station
New York, NY 10113

www.nyqbooks.org

First Edition

Set in New Baskerville

Layout and Design by Raymond P. Hammond
Cover Photo: Holger Spiering/ Westend61/Getty Images

Library of Congress Control Number: 2009928754

ISBN: 978-1-935520-02-3

Songs from an Earlier Century

Acknowledgments

Grateful acknowledgment is made to the editors of the following journals in which these poems first appeared: "Dawn, Chatham, Massachusetts," *The Worcester Review;* "In a Lovely Vineyard By the Lake," *The New Hampshire Review;* "The Art of the Night," Inkwell; "Over the Harlem River," *Entelechy, International;* "*Vita Beata,*" Ridgefield Magazine; "Intrusion," "The Constancy of Pines," "No Retreat," and "A Finish," *The New York Quarterly.*

For Shelly. Я люблю тебя.

Contents

Songs from an Earlier Century

The Stars

We must forgive ourselves
for being human.
And thank the stars
we are.
How dull to be a god.
Some people believe in you.
Most don't.
Being here is the stuff of faith.

Conspiring

The uneasy air shudders
at the talk in the trees.
A gutteral grumble,
a whispered threat,
a behind-the-hand alert
hissed in menace
by a villain wind
over the stricken snow,
too spent, too flecked with dirt
to cool the strands of air
that weave the afternoon gray.
To hear them tell it,
there's hell in the storm to come.

The Wind and a Leaf

In a parking lot
the wind skittered a leaf
over the stones.
At the side of my sight
it looked like a mouse,
a fat, brown mouse,
dragging a tail-like stem.
Then, the wind flipped it
on its back.
For a moment, I forgot
it was a leaf.
And I thought
it wanted me
to scratch its belly.

Dawn, Chatham, Massachusetts

The sea skips a wind through the curtains.
Outside our lodging-house room, the Russian

gardener hoses lilies and hanging-down
mums. Birds, wind-stuttered leaves and the sun

still wet from the ocean tear from morning
scraps of unused night, dissolving stars.

Tires rattle the gravel in the drive.
Light swatches jiggle beneath the maples.

All we need to chart a course to noon,
afternoon and every night beyond

is breathing, touching love
day-simmered and wrested from the dark.

Wet Sunday

The crackling storm
sprays the night
outside my car.
The lights juggle
the roiling air;
picking out
each drop racing
like a panicked atom.
The black trees finger
the black clouds
and rake rain
from the bulging sky.

Haying

Sweat stings the scratches on his arms.
He bumps on bales as the wagon

Creeps wavy down from the shorn slope.
Ducking 'neath an oak limb he tears

A leaf green and veined, torn to cool
His swollen hand. All the morning

He's hefted hay by hairy twine
Raking flesh, burning sunned muscles.

The rusty tractor barked and whined.
The baler beat time chomping grass

Into spriggy blocks. Now they ride
The clover scent from the sunfield

To dark mow to wait for winter
And the mouth of a cow. Spiders

In the barn ready webs that look
Like caught fog, like an angel's thoughts.

For its cricket-sugar he bites
A green sprig. Looking back, he squints

At sun glaring on the cropped field,
The hill trees, the heat-wiggled roof

Of the barn. He bumps atop bales.
He's scratched and aching and hoping

A summer hope for spring water
Dipped by a dipper dented, gray

From that bulging barrel sitting
And seeping in maple tree shade.

In a Lovely Vineyard By the Lake

I'm shaking. I push my nose
into the cold, clotted dirt,
hairy and smelling like wind in a cave.
My stomach and legs grind into the ground.

A man yells — I see a smudge of moon
thin and white along his gun barrel, still smoking
and aimed above the ditch where I lie.
Apparently, he owns the grapes I've stolen.

In September at the shore
of this good lake are the good grapes,
heavy, blue-clouded
and waiting to be conquered

by a farmer or a thief.
He has a hoe, a rake, shears to snip
the crippled vine. And a gun.
I only have a sack from the grocery

where I bought bread and cheese
and spicy slices of meat and where,
if I'd known I'd be shot at in a vineyard,
I would've bought grapes.

Intrusion

As I loll burned by words a poet wrote
Spear-topped pines stab a storm, warm and splotching.
There's rain and wind but no alerting note
That this sky is deviling, needs watching
And it slyly slips lower quite quiet.
The rascally clouds bump and break and spill
(I am not prepared, I'll not deny it)
On me, on my book; they spill where they will.
The strangling damp glowers all in a haze
And thickens and dims day around me;
It shrouds yellows and greens with wet grays
Halting my reading, killing it soundly.
Closing my book, I tuck it under my shirt
And slog through rude rain muddying the dirt.

What is Winter Up To?

Yellow light from my neighbor's kitchen slides
over the ice-hard snow and piles against
my porch empty of the will to borrow
a cup of something. The sky holds to the earth
in the black stitches of trees, just tight enough
to tear holes that look like stars. The air
pinches cold on my ears; I listen for it
to break. Snow-poke maps drawn by children
and deer carve the yard into icy
vacant nations. Tire-chains muffle-ching
from the road banks peppered with sand and salt.
I smell the snow. It steals from the air pieces
of any sound and buries them in the lumped
white ridges. And there the pieces wait
for the distant hiss of spring.

In the Cold

Winter twists the woman's black hair
around her face. She hugs
her arms tight to the top of her coat.

The street lamp sparks the frost orange
and shows the woman's lips straight and taut,
her eyes, scraped by the tangle of her hair,

wobble in the wide white around them.
Winter flaps the bottom of her coat,
baring her legs to the street lamp light.

Her boots work over the snow,
crunching it. Across the street, on a knoll,
the church, in its brick cassock,

stands between stolls of leafless oaks.
The woman defies the wind
as it grabs at her coat and coughs frost

into her worry. And across the street
the colored glass eyes of the church
wait for a candle to be lighted.

That Holy Moment

Snow shakes from pillows
bumping the hills,
torn by trees and blessed
not to be window panes.

Snow in the morning
too thin to hold its white
between the sun and the sidewalk,
a cold smoke.

Snow fills the air
and won't allow proud ancestors,
reduced to dust, above to walk
and weigh and peer.

Does the snow fall?
Or froth up in prayer
prayed in that holy moment
before sleep?

The Homeless Wind One Recent Night

The homeless wind one recent night
Came slipping down the tree-filled hill
And fluffed the leaves with sound so slight
It came scarce past my window sill.

Autumn was in that August eve
And autumn in my house and heart.
Sun and summer had taken leave.
My thoughts were thoughts of those who part.

All hushed and dark, a time asleep
And the curling leaves stirred a bit
As eyes do when our dreams are deep.
I prayed the wind would never quit.

A Fire

The air tries to settle
from the ripping siren
that chased the truck out of Annville.
The bikes of boys
scratch the gravel.

In the firehouse the truck left,
shopkeepers and a stagger-over
from the tap room
lump before the blackboard
on the cinder-block wall:

"Castner Farm. Bedient Hill."
The chalked words look like smoke confessing.
The boys drop their bikes,
rear tires spinning,
and squeeze through the elders

talking-up Bedient Hill, wondering
if the Castner cows were in the barn
or grazing in the fly-buzz field.
From the blackboard the boys trade hopes
the fire is not too far

and not too steep for bicycles.
The sun keeps pulling the day along.
The elders wander back to their shops
and spirits. Sad headshakes
for the cows and the Castners and Bedient Hill.

But the boys stay at the firehouse
until dusk and loss drag the volunteers back.
From a house and a farm
stolen by smoke
the color of chalk.

Vita Beata

A wren speaks
of yesterday's just-cut
grass. A finch chortles
at the climbing sun.
Day cannot bear the weight
of any more night.
It lightens up its load.
The morning moon bends
before the church of earth
and weaves a breeze
through hazel leaves
still young enough
in foliage and faith
to think they will
never die
ever.

A Crackling of Thorns

March maples moan
at the rude wind

raking grass still patched
with snow.

I commit the sin of despair.
Spirit pales; eyes purple

in a fog dimming, dragging,
dooming. In the cave

of lost looks and shackled
shadows, hangs a prickling

gray, drunk mist.
Twisted, crippled limbs

reaching for rescue,
stop...stunted, done.

I sit and I stare
committing the sin of despair.

Waiting

A red toolbox sits on the stone
that served as a step for seventy years
to the porch of the house
by the train station.
The house is beginning to bend
from the weight of the moss
on its roof.
I dance from foot to foot,
waiting for the train
and watch my breath
rag into the blue air.
For seventy years
the house has heard
the ping-song in the tracks
of the coming train.
The early orange of winter evening
glows through the upstairs window.
The toolbox and a coil of cord
the color of the sky
wait on that cold, stone step
below the porch that bows.
Did cigar ashes and spots
of spilled tea fill the years
with such a weight
that it sags the porch
before the door, that's now
just a plywood plug?
It had to be more than winter
that dulled the yard
to seeping grey thistles and burrs.

Horses must once have stood waiting,
bending a hoof,
where saw-horses lean now,
on the toolbox and cord.
My ears redden in sliding-down day.
I turn from the house
and look up the track,
hoping to see the white light
round and growing
of the wide, warming train,
the white light throwing silver spears
in all directions.
When the train comes, I'll go.
But the old house will wait.
For the workers and the tools.
And when they come to it,
when they come to the house,
will they be working to bring it back?
Or working to bring it down?

The Sky in the Narrows

Fitful winter is dying,
never having come of age.

No protest, no flailing
Ghostly arms; no snow,

no cracking cold, only leaves,
abandoned to the dark.

Above trees narrowing the road,
the lopped-off moon lines silver

on the jagged rags of clouds;
clouds like continents uncharted

on the ocean of the sky
in the dusty distance of time.

Lake Effect

Tuesday exploded choking
cold. Wind slithered snakes
of snow over Erie Street
and curled horse-tails
from the roofs.
And as the day burst,
light, itself, fell apart
into pieces that failed to glow,
failed to glow,
and only hung
dulling in the air.

Islands of the Night

In the tangle of time
Through bare branches,
Clouds lie
In the black sky
Stretched and thinned
By the wind.
The clouds part
From the moon; then,
Cover the moon,
Taking the moongift glow
Ragged continents show.
Port of ghosts,
Harbored rememberings.
Longing of belonging
On the sparkle and ice
In the black sky,
These mapped only tonight
Islands streak like a fox,
Like a sung song,
Like a kiss in the pines,
Pulled to wavy, hazy gauze.
Who peoples those clouds?
Ragged farmers
And factory hands?
Wives who fell through love
To death and drink?
Sons shivering hope
Out of their hearts
And daughters who put down
More than dolls?

On the ragged islands
Mapped on this night
Do names turn to curses?
Or do they polish
In the vapored wind
And join the sparkle
Of stars?
Clouds lie
In the black sky,
Ragged, bright,
Mapped only tonight.
They dim the moon,
Its middle-night threads
Of fabric islands
Of unreachable beaches
Of hills that surround
Valleys one moment,
Then sink to become them
The next.

Storm Overture

I only need the small death breath
of lilacs beside a peeling
wall to ride upon sunny dust
to the top of the round maple.
I only need to sit alone on a slope
above town.
I only need to rise up blue rags
in a climbing cumulous cloud
like shadows on snow.

Thunder from the darkening side
of the hilly trees comes spying.
Cicadas spin their rattling fence of song.
The little dog sleeps. A child sits
in the clover lawn and he knows
without learning that the storm will storm.
And he'll think of this forever.

Last Poem

The Berkshire wind beneath oak leaves asks
what will be the last poem I shall read?
Under god-green trees stuttering summer,
saying old things, what words will be
the last I shall read?

A poem about a boy too far from town to learn
baseball? A cowherd seeing by a lighted rush,
his tongue to be touched by fire? Will a barbarian yawp
or a slender fellow in the grass be
the last I shall see?

Might time stop as I climb from a repaired watch
or an extraordinary evening east
of this Connecticut town in that wind
beneath those leaves? Will I die for lack
of what I might have found?

Could I be waiting for the distant day
in the last poem I shall read?
Might my eyes close as I close the book
of an ode to a nightingale? to fall?
a midnight frost? a stolen boat?

When I fear no more the heat of the sun
or a dizzy whiskey waltz, will I read
the last, the lost, the million-moon river
that parted to hark the wine-stained
thrush coming in from the dark?

Do You Demand Praise?

Do you demand praise?
I suppose you do from some psalm.
But the man as flesh as I
orders me to praise you.
And I do. In his words. Not mine.
In his church. Not mine.
I hear the trees
susurrating nights and days
In the wolf-wise wind,
gathering soul dust
on its never resting rounds.
That is where I hear praise
or wish to offer it:
to the wind, to the trees,
to the tumbling clouds
living twice: in the orbiting sky
and the juddering pond.
Praise as mystery, as secret,
offered as hope, not fact.
Will you accept that praise?
Will you look upon me
in patience, in knowing
I am finished with asking.
I am working on accepting.
Your distance. My place
under trees, in clover breeze
juggling light like laughter.

Goldenrod

The tasseled yellow
at the top of laddered leaves

vexes autumn with defiant
summer. Boys harvested

an acre's eighth of goldenrod,
wove their crop into forts

and slew each enemy other
until time for supper.

Two girls built beds for babies
whose plastic eyes closed for naps.

Now the sun aims an angled heat,
leaving the shadeside cooler.

And the knobby, peeling stalks
stand straight in the pleasure

of opened school,
closed porch doors

and fattened woodchucks gone below
to gather sleep for winter.

Incubus

Summer will ghost out of a rip
in the wallpaper
or vapor from cobblestones
beside the creek. Summer
curls the covers of books.
It whispers from the leaves
of maple trees, all wrinkled
trunks and crippled limbs.
It breathes upon your sleeping.
With a white hot light
summer tears its cloth clouds
and hangs them ragged in the sky
to drop rain on this hot, haunted earth.
And all of that,
all of summer threading
and weaving and wetting
the heavy air,
odors up the dark.

Up North

In the frigid middle of Sunapee Lake
a smokey-ghost wind works the surface

like a mason's apprentice hurrying
to smooth ...and failing. Clouds race

and bump and pull shadows over aspens,
through beeches and scud in the iron water.

On the rock-stocked shore the pines are urgent,
maples chatter, poplars cough

and rattle; but it's all tree-talk
flannel folks don't understand.

They ignore the wind warning,
Stay in. Stay in. Out of the spirit-mad air.

Green Leaves Agitate the Hill

Green leaves agitate the hill,
catching and juggling the sun.

A cloud shadow rakes and rasps
like a ghost of clocks.

I pray at the window
to that ghost. Pray to fly fading

into the juddering May leaves
on the sun-stumbled hill.

Warning

Tonight I crossed Pennsylvania.
As I drove deeper into dark
a storm spat at me: it shook my car
and me. Lightning offered up
the ragged sky. Coal-full hills
black as coal. Up ahead a bolt,
thick and silver white,
licked my sight and burned
a ten-minute scar
in the back of my eye;
it glowed when I blinked.
I was driving
from New York to Ohio,
but Pennsylvania ranted.
Rain, lightning,
and the wobble of the wind
sent a clouded message completely clear:
don't cross Pennsylvania.

July

I walked last night in the Annville woods.
Ghostly and shadowed and green:
A buffeted, bothered green:
Like the smoke of envy.
I hiked in swirling, misted minutes
Thinking of thinking of nothing.
The wind was a glory,
It raked the rain horizontal.
Today the calm is back
With heat like that from beneath
An old, tired tent.

Something I Could Not Tell You

I wanted the hill more than home
and fevered guilt rose with my wanting.
I wanted the hill of dripping daisies and moss;
a soft stalk of hay to chew to green juice.
I wanted to climb the hill
and force the village far and down,
and laugh from that high green place;
no trace of grief or trembled remembering.
You wore out with work, ending your day and days
tired, shrunk, drunk, frowning, glowering, dead.
I wanted the hill and a twitchy hound
a white-tipped tail, a pillow, a yip;
to only stalk butterflies and woodchuck holes.
I wanted the hill and a leaf-curled book
of maidens and forests and kings.
Kings who killed; kings who blessed
the page and broke the holy snow.
I wanted the hill more than home.

Lunartude

Bless you, Moon,
for pouring light
on the needles of the quieted pine.
For your sky milk
in the sacred night.
For green breath
and swamp glow,
for the spirited rite,
bless you, Moon.

Something In It

This wind this day scrapes
down the stone-piled years.
It breathes hoarse, as if through pines.
What does it tow? A collie's bark?
The scent of a farm?
Manure and sausage and hay?
Does the wind creak a rope
swaying from a beam
in the mow to the wagon-wide door,
crazing the chaf in the sun?
Does this wind lump
underfoot the dirt-road stones?
Does it bear stories clacked
by a wrinkle-faced woman
of arrow-heads in boxes and shells
from a dreamed-of ocean?
Are there stories of Gettysburg
and Lincoln and dust settling
on the torn wool cloak up
in the attic? Does it carry
the night a hobo came out
of the cellar, clomped through
the parlor, fleeing in the domestic dawn?
This wind writes
in the tops of the trees
and fills the day with more
than trees and day can hold.

The Lost Poem Project

It makes no sense. Disappearing without
as much as a dusty wisp, or settling

notes of air, of falling, smalling sounds.
I'd thought I had it in my palm, my fingers

curling confidently. Ready to tuck it
away. Then, I discovered it was gone.

I felt my eyes grow damp. What do you mean...gone?
I had it. How could that be? Now, what?

Do I tip back down the years? To that night
my father smashed through the garage door?

To find it must I go flipping, flailing
and tossed to land in Annville village before

they cut down the trees? In that scrufty
upstate town? In the lodge halls and pool halls

and school halls where we were when we heard
Kennedy was shot and we talked about

thumbing down to Washington to join the line
by his coffin, to try to clear our stunned,

numbed wonder? Or was it lost in the shoulder-
to-shoulder farce of a draft physical

when seventy-three army-alarmed strangers
shivered in our underwear on the third floor

of the federal building in Buffalo?
Oh, damn! I lost it somewhere back, back, back,

back then. Or there. Somewhere. Maybe it was when
I was twelve and jumped out the church window,

grass-stained my pants and annoyed the hell
out of some old Methodist named Myrtle,

if she had any hell left. She told my
father. She told Reverend Kane. She even told

that lady who smoked non-filters and knew
my mother. Or did it disappear the night

we partied in the pines up on Kahler Hill
and dove into the needles on the ground

when the sheriff deputy roared up
out of the dark and flashed the lights and hit

the sirens and swore. A swear is a curse
and a curse will take it, steal it faster

than a crook at the county fair. Or maybe
it was there. The county fair. When Herbie

went for vinegared fries and came back drunk.
Yes, it might have been at the county fair.

It isn't fair, but gone it is. Gone, lost,
stolen, tossed. I had it in my hand,

right in my palm, but now it isn't here.
When I learned it was gone I felt like dying.

Skipping A Stone

Wait for the wind
to stop riffling the pond.
Then, lean with your arm
and fling a flat stone
from the curve between
your thumb and finger. Stand
and watch it skip.
It denies it's heavier
than the water. It won't go
straight away; but in a curve
from its launch
to the left
on dotted hops
that shorten with each between.
The stone curves
from its launch
to the left
and sinks
trying to
come
back.

Snow

Tonight the first snow falls.
It stirs me in the black back
of my mind. I see it through
my reading glasses and feel
the grainy sled-tremble.
My ears burn blue with the cold.
I remember I worshiped
the snow enough
to eat it like a sacrament.
In the morning I'll press
my palm against the window and
melt a hole
in the holy frost
to see how white is the day.

Inevitable

The confused bramble
(maples, oaks, beeches,
birches and dogwood) is kept
from the sloping meadow
by a straight break of pines.
It must have been sweet
to the hawk's eye
when she lifted to look.
And sweet to the ear of the deer
when the wind whispered
at sunset. But, the rake is rusted.
It sinks into the brown bent grass
that failed to make one more hay.
The farmer hobbled off the field,
climbed the leaning porch
and pulled off his rubber boots
marbled with mud and dung.
The boots cooled and dried
his sweat from the second cutting
into the last cutting.

The Smoke of Time

A dark photograph
in the Annville Hub.
A high school cast on a stage
poses in a play eighty years ago.
You stare from a wicker chair
in the picture's left,
your eyes large, lashed and aimed
at where I wish I were.
Who is it you see?
Oh, I fancy you see me; but, you don't.
What is it you see?
Some coming color?
A hand to hold? Missed kisses?
From behind the footlights
and the curtain drawn aside,
in your shaped, dark dress
and lace collar, your hair
curving to your shoulder,
sweet hands upon your lap,
what is it you see across eighty years?

The circus lumbering away from summer
taking small smiles
and the smell of horses and dust?
Do you look into dreams?
Those of that actor in the bow tie?
Dreams of a brother?
A brother killed in France?
Do know in your dreams that Abe
will marry the woman who never smiles?

Do you see your shining hair dulling
like a cloud raked by a wind?
What is it you see?
What is it you know?
In the old photograph
are you frozen in time?
Or frozen in fear?
At what you see
through the smoke of time?

The Art of the Night

I rise and fall along the air of aging,
dreams sharpen and draw clearer.

Night is lined and colored full-raging.
I twirl through smells of cinnamon, beef,

and a breathing girl. A willow droops
with day's leaving light; its roots crease the backs

of my legs, dent my arms. Thin, long leaves
play with the stars I see between and try to reach,

as I rise and fall along the air of aging
and try to touch stars in the odd purple sky.

What will I bump and brush
in the dusty dark? A dead blacksmith

taking shape again and frowning?
In these hilly, wooded dreams will I see

a money-worried woman throwing dishwater
from a battered tin pan and feeding a beagle

killed by a car? Do the lines draw boys growing
into wrinkled workers with drink-joggled eyes?

And girls who only remember songs; but, cease,
themselves, to sing? These lines in my dreams

sharpen and draw clearer
as I rise and fall along the air of aging.

Making Plans

Might a gentle Connecticut hill
Serve as my burying place?

Please, not a little valley
Where vaporous spirits

Sink and soak and make
The overalled worker crazy,

But a soft fair field knoll,
Under willows, under birches,

Beneath goldenrod, parted and marked
By the shy, twilight deer;

Where cricket autumn chirrs
The air 'til ghostly snow tufts

Upon the twigs. A quiet nutmeg slope
Where spring unpacks a picnic

On the waving, windy green;
Sprouts buttercups, daisies,

And Queen Anne's lace. May I hear
The wind speak secrets

Deep into sleeping
Forever for keeping;

Forever and gentle
On a hidden Connecticut hill.

Stranger Snow

Snow attacks
from a place far
and foreign.

Invading with a stark,
winded weight,
it looks like

a worried fur
to blur the inch
above the molded

white mounds,
a snarl
in the sewn,

sifted crystals
that prick the cheek
and click the window.

There's more breakage
than season, when
the season comes to March.

Mass

He kissed his book.
With rain dropping from the eaves,
eavesdropping,
in God-gone November,
he lifted his book
to a level with his eyes
and like a priest at the gospel
bent his neck in supplication.
In the crease between the pages
he nosed the odored ink
and kissed black words
into what he called his soul.

Under the Roof Lines Of Annville

Summer hangs a haze,
Dimming the green burble
Of leaf-tops and
The reaching steeples of Annville.
Summer holds the sun
Behind a thin, brown drape,
Holds it from sinking.
Somewhere under the arrested
Air a bartender pours gin
For a red-faced teacher
In a prickling gray suit.
A surgeon cuts
A mole
From the nose
Of a boy's aunt.
A boy who remembers every
Story she told him —
How a woman she knew
Could shudder a table
Without touching it.
And when her grandfather
Came home maimed
From Gettysburg.

There is a lawn sloping
South into dandelions
And shade
Piled
At the bottom.
I miss lying there

In the soft bug-buzz
Trying to make something
Of the sky, of the night.
Ice cream lumps
Melting in a dish;
Ice cream about to be eaten
By a girl in a leg brace.
She limps
From the private car
That drives her
To a school with stone walls
And paper silhouettes
In the windows.
A gray sedan whistles
The corner pavement, scaring
Three sparrows
From Elm Street
To an elm tree
Whose leaves don't wave,
Don't notice.
In a leaning house
The sun through
The parlor window catches
The summer dust
When old Leta holds
A glass of beer
The doctor prescribed
For her heart.
Day holds heat
In the curtains.

Out on the sparkled sidewalk
A bicycle lies
With a ball glove
Strapped on the handle bar;
The wheel keeps
Spinning;
And grease boils
On the back axle.
At the movie house
Cranston, the projectionist,
Unpacks a film
About a bad lawyer
With squinty eyes
And a three-piece suit.
The film will glow
In the faces of row-bound
Women in blue blouses.
Men circle sunburned arms
About the shoulders
Of the young women.
I circled shoulders
Once and willed my hands
To warm and comfort
And touch.
And under
The roof lines
Of Annville
Summer gives the trees
The look
Of a stalled, drooped groan.

The steeples stop
Short of that
For which they reach,
Arrested, frozen
In the summer-thick
Haze.

Kahler Hill

The climb up Kahler Hill narrows
between the crowding, lighting leaves.

God! how sweet is this sight and scent.
The tar-ey and gravel road climbs

to the greened top of the county
to look down upon hayfield farms,

their pastures and maples and pines.
To look down upon distant dots

of silent, chewing Holstein cows
and stalled cars unrusted, unheard.

Is the air on my hair and face
a spirit from this high kingdom

come up with me to remember
those we left lost and loved below?

Through this soft, happy haze I see
the hands-on-hips girl hasn't aged

into her wrinkled widowhood;
the dreaming boy is slim and brisk,

able still to throw a baseball
to save a sorrow from growing.

And the way-below roads are like
woven gray rivers slowed and stilled

and just listening to the years.
Look down upon the dim village

silent, sunned, and all people-housed,
lawns below quilt-like and quiet.

I am happy here on this hill
washed by all the sparrow-singing.

Happy beside shaded wren-routes
through maple trees and ivy vines,

with their fluttering and swaying
from wise wandering winds saying

their old and glowing secrets
reaching this sacred, heavened height.

Sunny Dust

After the rain
of the night before,

after shuddering thunder,
after cedars taken

in the anger of heaven,
this *day* is soft.

Sun settles
with the little wind that,

trying to steal
the leaves,

merely makes them stutter.
The wind threads

my window screen,
leaving the sun

in a dust
on the wire.

Night the Color of Coffee

If I could will a world
I'd will a narrow street
of tree-fronted buildings, planter-boxes,
awnings and vapor lights
spreading amber cones
down to the sidewalk.
I'd will the night
cold stormy. Alone
in a coffee shop I'd read
the work of my day. Beyond
the window wind would shatter
the routes of the snow
into twists and rises
and falling and wobbles,
in a thick, white scribble
of a god gone mad,
gone howling,
gone.
I'd loll in the cafe
just a window away
from night the color of coffee.
And my home-in-waiting
would be a walk-up flat
with books and the steam
of a stew on the stove.
Just a snow-swirled
blue walk
through the storm,
through the window
from the cafe in the night.

The Wind Outside the Window

The wind outside the window roils
leaves against leaves. It preaches

freedom in black rustling night,
stirring leaves against leaves.

In the dark, spirits *see* the wind I hear.
In the dark, darker trees bubble and bulge

And shrink against themselves.
Spirits call courage from hiding;

a courage I can't quite clutch
in my curling, closing fingers.

Revealing

Black branches weave
in the green leaves.
This cedar has come
to summer.
Weak spring's droop
is gone.
A rude wind lifts
the taut, full season
and looks beneath
to show the sky
black branches woven
in the green leaves.

One

Rain catches light.
And the soft song
Of its falling
Moves the tree,
The wren
And me.

Spirits

After an ice storm
Wind in the trees.
Listen: window taps
Of little ghost children
Faintly haunting
The cold.
Faintly failing
To be anything
But heard.

Song From An Earlier Century

We must come from a different place
for our ear to hold a sound.
To catch a difference from what we know
we need be born away.
A hundred years ago, in another town
a wood house sits
by the dirt road close enough
for wagon-wheeled dust to settle
on the lace curtain. On the porch,
her hair parted in the middle, wearing
the long, full dress and a bacon-stained
apron is Annie, humming and sweeping
in time to the tune. Her hair can't hold
the place the comb combed it.
A strand unlocks and rides
on the stirred air of her sweeping.
She doesn't watch her work,
doesn't watch the floor,
her eyes are on the hill beyond
the sun-browned window. And over it,
over the hill, just past the crooked,
black apple orchard, a man old enough
to shave but hasn't, wearing wool
and sweating, chops bird's-foot trefoil
for his rabbits out back.
His cheeks are tanned beneath
a lined, white brow. Owen, he's called,
and he's singing, too. The woman with the broom
and the sickle-swinging man sew that day
with notes: a song from an earlier century.

There's always a hill, always work or frowning.
Always between them. His old man can't spare
an hour or a coin or a small, good word.
With her father buried some seven years
her mother lies up a-bed ...shriveling, coughing,
and with wet, dim eyes, looking over the window-sill
for death.
Annie wants books and college.
Owen wants Annie.
Their song ripples the air with waves
that *still*, after a hundred years, plow
the universe. Throat-born, heart-born song
from two sides of a hill
still slip away and graze the hourless miles.
We need be born away
from what we come to know.

Wearing Out

On spring's first warm day clouds grip a puffed clump
at the limb-cracked horizon. Sun reddens
my head and a gift-green breeze dries the sweat.
The urge to lose winter comes from wooly
weariness and that urge builds an urgency.
No matter how late or deep winter takes
a poke at these hills, it's a swing swung
by a losing, staggered bully. The warm,
the rain and the rilling will wash the leaving,
bleeding season down the ground, down the rocks,
and down to the seagull sea.

Sun and Wind and Web

An empty cobweb droops
from where the branch
joins the trunk.
The spider is gone,
its flies and moths devoured.
Sun and sudden wind
team to flutter the web,
to sparkle it
with breath and light.
Sun and wind and web
meet, tremble
and move morning
into something living.

The Moon Kept the Oaks

With quick dread just below my heart
I thought I caught a bat
whiffling this moon-foggy night.
A bat's not seen,
it's remembered,
and tears a scratch in the sky.
I'll believe the bat was there.
But I *know* the moon was;
and it kept the oaks sketched
upon the fog.

Near Annville

Foggy dawn curtains the trees
upon hill, upon hill,
their leaves like hushed, praying monks
and day just comes.
It doesn't settle or rise
or ride a beam.
Day just comes
cottoned, grey,
insubstantial,
a ghost, a mist,
so humid-crowded
it permits
only me.
And early, wet,
unwound twilight
glows
upon hill, upon hill.

Unseasonable

This enlightened day
could not be clearer.
Sunned, summer leaves,
jostled by the wind,
hold aloft the blue,
the steady,
smooth blue.
The sun loses itself
to the little wind,
to the billion leaves,
loses itself, breaks and falls.
And in the air
between sun and sight
dandelion puffs dance
like a crazy, lost snow.

The Place He Chose

On the muddy March slope
you crumble the earth
with your determined green growth.
You spear, you frond, you blade, you grass.
April steals brown winter
and sleight-of-hand budding
grows leafy and damp.
You reach, you rise, you grow, you seek,
seek the sun, riding its east-west dome;
you take the gild into your delicate stalk
of sugar and strength and wind-bend
to become June field, to become July hay,
to become crop, to become food
to sit in the dark barn mow
where Eben Tolley will stand
one August morning
with a pheasant gun his grandfather gave him.
Where he'll blast the chaff from the rafters
as the shot rips the side of his head
to a sticky red seeping on the hay
drying and cooling and waiting
for Thursday to find him
there on you, the just-cut hay,
you that grew in the field
that came to the barn
to feed the cows.
Cows, who now
will be sold
or butchered
to pay
for
things.

Talk

Two wives click over
the summer sidewalk
into the coffee shop.
With husbands trained
away to the city
they set the plastic
baskets
with their sleeping babies
on the floor
by the tables.
The wives talk
of locks
on contemporary doors;
of carpet and spilling
and how good it is
to be rid of gloves.
The red-haired wife
in her smooth blue
blouse talks
of town,
this August heat,
soap and
summer's end.
Blowing out a breath,
the other wife,
in white from shoulder
to shoe, scratches
one thigh, narrows
her eyes
and looks to the side

hoping the neighbor
table can't hear.
Out on the street
cars thrum
and the silly leaves
flutter. The wives
laugh and wonder
about "a friend"
no longer amusing,
no longer part
of their coffee-odored
hours. One crosses her legs
and pushes dark glasses up
in her hair. The rings
on the other's fingers are silver;
the nails on both wives are red.
With all the heat — of summer,
of bedrooms,
of hating the trips
to the A and P — the air
around them
chills with talk
of school
and the cost of clothes.
And words
pile on the table between
like snow.

Over the Harlem River

The odd blue-grid bridge drifts closer
and the train, like some great lake boat,
floats into Manhattan. The pillow-hid
rumble of the track *sounds*
how the leaves on the trees *look*:
soft and lumped and slowly tossed
in a wind that's filled with summer.
Above brick tenements birds stitch
the clouds and keep the sky from falling
on the city. The train stretches
all this, all this I see, from the blue
railroad bridge to the tunneling
Grand Central dark to soot
and work and empty suits losing
light in the many bounces from
window to window and down on the street.

Franconia

Is it the burden of words
or the tread of ghosts buckling

the old house down?
Is it a kneeling before that father

mountain across the valley?
A bow, an aimed-down gaze, an awe?

What bends this peeling house?
What nods it, graves it gray

to a look of supplication?
I sense a musty smile, amusement

in the beams and year-cracked rafters.
This house in which a poet left

a sunny dust of verse,
of words lodged and tossed away.

He piled splintered thoughts
high on a New Hampshire hill.

Stride of Time

Whitened old man wades in the English hay
and high daisies of a Dymock field,
a field he'd hiked when young. When his wife lived

and her hair always wisped from its clip.
Their looks slipped day and night a warm good.
Their children blurred in running.

Now clouds drag him and the hills with rolling shadows,
from hedge-row to the valley grass, tumbling
to rest beneath the trees. He remembers

his wife and their children and a Welsh friend
who took a shell in the neck in the war.
Whitened old man sees them, sees them all

in the broken shade beneath the trees.
And coming here in so large a stride of time
is a stick that stirs the grief time had banked.

Near November

In mid-night the underside
of the cloud is a ragged lightened gray.
I imagine the un-caved air
above it; and the work of the moon:
silvering the top,
sparking the ice,
teaching stars how to night.
But on the earth
wind wrestles weak October,
steals grieving leaves,
flattens its grass,
and streaks the trees with rain.

The Task

Wind draws through the trees,
rattling shingles,
shaking something
from silence.
The wind rakes over the snow
and cuts it, bleeding cold
back into the gray air,
back into the brown grass,
back into trees and limbs
stiff and moaning
for the green things
of far spring.

Two Loves

It rained
all the foggy morning
flooding
the woods
behind my house.
I love the rain.

Now, the sun,
sinking down to night,
casts on my curtains
shadows of the pines
like fingers
flexing the wind.
Wet, glistening, waving.
I love the sun.

Storm in a Street Lamp

The snow rants,
slanted, slashing
in the light.

A car-shaking wind
from the bursting heart
of the night throws the snow

like executioner stones,
like battle arrows,
like rage.

The storm bullies
and shakes
every corner and crack,

and I tremble seeing it
in the orange glow cone
of the swaying street lamp.

No Retreat

If I leave my darkening porch
I leave rain and playing thunder
for the door, for the house.
I leave leaf-powdered breath,
calmed trees and unfearing flowers.
I leave wet wood, misty shingles,
pattling drops on the awning.
If I leave this day, dimmed now to night,
for the dry inside and ovened beef,
I leave the lawn rejoicing
in the love of drink,
freed from the weight of sun
wiggling the yellow air.
I leave squirrel and napping fox.
I leave a creek parading by cowslips,
a creek singing to silenced, listening wrens.
I leave patches of sky
aged from blue to black.
If I retreat from this sweet porch
for carpets and couches
and table-clothed tables
I'll sit and think about tea.
If I leave now, I leave loved rain
and miss the song of the returning wren
when the rain stops.

Two Fields

I waded through two fields today.
The first an Annville meadow.
Sun and breeze
fluffed the leaves
of ringing maples and oaks.
Light landed yellow on the swaying hay,
which lifted and begged
of the morning more.

That sight took me to another field.
Up a creek-bank, soddy, tufted
behind a flat, grayed house.
To a lumped orchard on a slope,
a crooked forest crippled by apple-birth.
Can-kicking an afternoon
after my paper route, I
stumbled over the autumn-fallen fruit,
tripping into thirst. I filled
my canvas bag with northern spies
and lugged the load to my porch.
In the slanting amber sun,
I crushed the stash
to cider. The bagful gave up
a glassful. Leaning against the
rail along the slanting boards,
I glared at the tumbler in my hand:
more sip in that harvest than drink.

The first field is here and glimpsed
in the automobile rush of late century.
I prayed to the god of the season,
that he stretch the moment, for me
to see it slow, to see it longer.
What he sent, in a remembered rush,
was the other field. Its appled
odor and bee buzz, its powdery wind
above a withered house
outside a shrinking, tippled town
I've not seen in a sigh of years.
And that older field bores through me still.

The Constancy of Pines

Wind in winter
slips down the frost-chilled hill
and brings icing in its coming.
Boughs sparkle and wave;
they're brittle and grave
even in the dancing, jeweled light.
Snow stays. Until it tumbles
to feathers in the grayed green.

Wind in spring
raises the dust of bud lust
with a greening in its coming.
Boughs shift from weight to light
and hold the host of the sun rite
broken and golden and blessed.
In memory rain-blacked bark drinks
from the chalice-like clouds.

Summer's wind
Speaks of grandfather farms,
dirt-roads, the heat of cows
in rippling, damp air
from the pasture to share
forces with a cottoning sky
to groan, to grumble, to thunder and rumble
over the pines and hilly oaks.

Then, autumn,
finally autumn and wind and pines
hold whispers and green
while the rest of the garden-giving world
rages and flares with angers unfurled
in unacknowledged dying, wrested death:
calming, drying, stopping, snuffed ends.
All but the needly trees which hallow the wind.

Threefall

The air blues high,
north of August.
Down it settles
cool and fogged,
closing windows.

The rain grays high,
born of a gust;
down it curls
in gales and smoke,
slamming doors.

The leaf golds high,
falling a must;
to show the oak,
to the covered ground,
the death of summer.

The Outside Wall Waits for Night

The outside wall waits for night to come home
from its rounds. An unclothed sun has stayed
all this spring day upon our outside wall,
angling from the window. As I look up
every page or so from evening reading,
I invite the night by watching for it,
Night lulls the drowsy wall with covers
and layers, one by one. All I have left
is a warmth in my face from being
outside. The wall is gray, but still defined,
still all wall (and I go back to reading).
A later glance betrays another change.
The wall dims dimension and it mingles
with a kitchen that looks like mine. The words
I read urge me on; I only stop
to notice the wall is finally gone.
And all I have for witness is the mirror-
image kitchen where the outside wall had been.

The Train Home After a Rain

Drops tremble
on the fence across the track.
I step from the train.
On the chain-link across the track,
the drops split
the station-house light.
With a whispy web above the gate
a spider asserts that eight legs
are smarter than six.
And the drops on the fence fall
nearly to earth.
They hold their place
on the wire,
above the mud,
above the rush to a storm grate.
The drops hold their place
to break the light
and wait
to take a slower leave.

Seeing

A gull stands sentry
on a steepled roof
high, still, wings close,
at attention.
Light gray gull against
dark gray sky
flying behind
the gull's un-flying,
many miles from the sea,
far from salt water
but close to me.
I see the gull
from where I stand.
And from where *he* stands
upon the steepled roof
above the slated ground
what he sees
is the sea.

A Finish

The day is so sunny and clear
the air looks like it could snap
and fall into small pieces
that would still sparkle
in what became
the end of the world.

About the Author

Ira Joe Fisher holds an MFA from New England College and has taught poetry at the University of Connecticut in Stamford, Pace University and New England College. He has lectured at the University of Connecticut, Stamford, Keene State College and Manhattanville College. His poetry has appeared in various literary journals and he is the author of *Remembering Rew* and *Some Holy Weight in the Village Air*, both of which are now in their second printings. Fisher has worked in radio and television for over forty years, most recently for the CBS *Early Show*. He has acted in films and on the New York stage (for many years appearing in *The Fantasticks*). He and his wife, Shelly, and their four children live in Connecticut.

About NYQ Books™

NYQ Books™ was established in 2009 as an imprint of The New York Quarterly Foundation, Inc. Its mission is to augment the *New York Quarterly* poetry magazine by providing an additional venue for poets already published in the magazine. A lifelong dream of NYQ's founding editor, William Packard, NYQ Books™ has been made possible by both growing foundation support and new technology that was not available during William Packard's lifetime. We are proud to present these books to you and hope that you will continue to support The New York Quarterly Foundation, Inc. and our poets and that you will enjoy these other titles from NYQ Books™:

Joanna Crispi	*Soldier in the Grass*
Ted Jonathan	*Bones and Jokes*
Amanda J. Bradley	*Hints and Allegations*
Fred Yannantuono	*A Boilermaker for the Lady*

Please visit out website for these and other titles:

www.nyqbooks.org

CPSIA information can be obtained
at www.ICGtesting.com
Printed in the USA
FSHW020359170819
61063FS

9 781935 520023